The Animal Kingdom

ANIMAL MIGRATION

Malcolm Penny

Illustrated by Vanda Baginska

The Animal Kingdom

Animal Adaptations
Animal Camouflage
Animal Defences
Animal Evolution
Animal Homes
Animal Migration
Animal Movement
Animal Partnerships
Animal Reproduction
Animal Signals
Animals and their Young
Endangered Animals
The Food Chain
Hunting and Stalking

Editor: Sue Bullen

First published in 1987 by
Wayland (Publishers) Ltd
61 Western Road, Hove
East Sussex BN3 1JD, England

© Copyright 1987 Wayland (Publishers) Ltd

British Library Cataloguing in Publication Data

Penny, Malcolm
Animal migration. — (The animal kingdom)
1. Animal migration — Juvenile literature
I. Title   II. Baginska, Vanda   III. Series
591.52'5   QL754

ISBN 0–85078–965–6

Typeset by DP Press, Sevenoaks, Kent, England
Printed and bound by Casterman SA, Belgium

Contents

The reasons for migration

Migration is the name given to regular movements of whole populations of animals from one place to another and back again, as conditions change. In the tropics, animals move in response to the dry season and rainy season. In the sea, small animals in the plankton migrate every day. As the sun rises, they sink deeper in the water because the sunlight is too bright for them. Later, as the daylight fades, they drift towards the surface again.

The most common form of migration, carried out by millions of animals every year, is into colder areas during the summer, and back to warmer parts of the world for the winter. Geese, for example, leave temperate countries in spring to fly north to the Arctic, often across stormy seas. Why do they take the risk? Like many birds, they go north to breed.

The map below shows the migration routes of some well-known migrants.

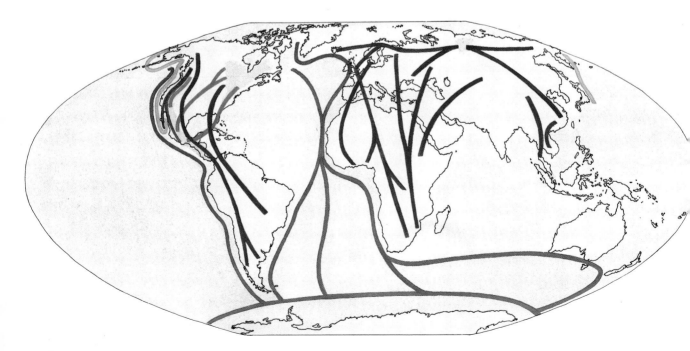

During the short Arctic summer, geese find plenty of food for their young, because few other animals live there all the year round. Also there is less danger from predators, compared with their winter homes. This is important for the adults as well, because they become unable to fly every summer, when they moult to grow new feathers.

Humans migrate, too. Nomadic tribes, such as the Bedouin, spend the dry season near oases in the Arabian Desert. In the rainy season they wander with their sheep and camels to find new grass for the animals. In northern Scandinavia, the Lapps follow their herds of reindeer north in summer and south again in winter.

All kinds of animals migrate – insects and birds fly thousands of miles over land and sea, whales and fish swim around the vast oceans, while herds of animals trek across the land. In this book we shall look at some of their amazing journeys.

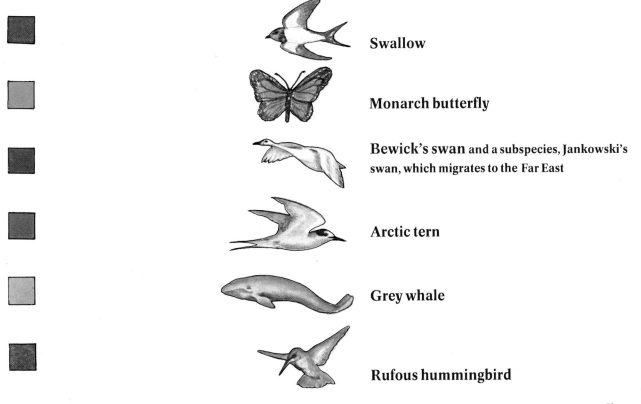

Swallow

Monarch butterfly

Bewick's swan and a subspecies, Jankowski's swan, which migrates to the Far East

Arctic tern

Grey whale

Rufous hummingbird

Timing the move

All over the world, people notice the migrations of animals, especially birds, and recognize them as signs of the changing seasons. Usually, the animals get it right: for example, as summer begins in the Northern Hemisphere, swallows fly from South Africa to Europe. Similarly, after spending the summer around the Arctic in order to breed, geese fly south to spend the winter in warmer areas. To time their movements so accurately, the birds must be alert to changes in their surroundings which may be too small for humans to notice.

Whatever the weather, the one thing which is the same in a particular place at a particular date is the length of time between sunrise and sunset. This is known as the 'daylength'. Almost every living thing is affected by daylength. This means plants as well as animals.

Daylength affects birds by making them restless when the days are getting longer in spring, or shorter in autumn. Nobody is really sure how it works, but they seem to become more sensitive to changes in the atmosphere at these times. As winter changes to spring, the air becomes warmer and the wind changes direction. Most of these changes are so gradual that humans do not notice them until after they have happened. The birds, however, are already on the move.

A European flower called the greater celandine, or swallow flower, opens at the same time as the swallows arrive. This is because the flower is responding to the same changes in daylength and temperature as the birds.

Opposite *Canada geese arrive at their wintering ground in the USA.*

6

Finding the way

When animals make long journeys across places where there is no food or shelter, such as deserts or oceans, it is very important that they should be able to navigate accurately.

Birds find their way by the stars at night, and by the sun during the day. People thought that this was impossible until some migrating birds were put in cages inside a planetarium. When the operator turned the artificial sky round, the birds gathered at the sides of the cages nearest to the direction in which they would have flown if the sky had been real. Every time he moved it, the birds moved to a new position. This proved that they could see the stars and respond to them.

Snow geese and sandhill cranes arrive in Bosque del Apache wildlife reserve in New Mexico to spend the winter.

However, a navigator must have an accurate clock, because the stars seem to move as the earth rotates.

Many animals, especially birds, have a very precise sense of time, which is called their 'internal clock'. In cloudy weather, birds delay setting off on long journeys, but if the cloud lasts for a long time, they must eventually go, to complete their migration in time. In such conditions, they are able to steer by following the magnetic field of the earth. We could say that they have their own special compass inside them, which tells them the right direction to go.

Most migrating animals travel in groups, sometimes in very large numbers. This makes it more likely that they will find the right way, especially when the group contains experienced animals which have made the journey before.

Thrushes and robins navigate by the stars. Pictured below are the European robin and song thrush.

The diagram below shows how a bird in a planetarium follows the stars, as the artificial sky is moved around.

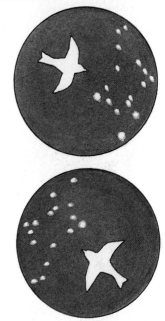

Swallows and ringing

People wondered for centuries where swallows went in the winter, when they disappeared from Europe. Some scientists believed that they hibernated!

Now their movements are quite well known, because some birds have been marked with lightweight metal leg rings, each stamped with a number. When a bird is caught again, or found dead, it is possible to find out when and where the ring was first put on.

The results show that before winter arrives, European swallows leave Europe and fly to South Africa, where it is summer. This is because South Africa lies in the Southern Hemisphere, which has summer when the Northern Hemisphere has winter. When spring returns in the Northern Hemisphere, they move northwards across Africa and the Mediterranean with the flow of warm air. The same species in North America, where it is called the barn swallow, avoids the northern winter by flying to South America, where it is summer.

Because the change of the seasons occurs at a slightly different time each year, the swallows return to the North on different dates. However, they arrive within the same two week period every year, in the second half of April. A pair of swallows uses the same nest site year after year.

There is a saying, 'one swallow doesn't make a summer'. This means that one or two birds often arrive before the main flocks, only to be caught out by late frost. Summer has truly begun only when the large flocks arrive.

Opposite *A flock of swallows arrive in late April to breed in Europe. The yellow flowers of greater celandine are already open.*

The map below shows the various migration routes of the monarch butterfly.

Migrating butterflies

The monarch, or milkweed butterfly, is well known for its amazing migration. In the town of Pacific Grove in California, USA, the people hold a street festival every winter, when the monarchs return from across the Canadian border in the north.

On the eastern side of Canada, the monarch butterflies set out on a much longer migration. Monarchs which breed as far north as Quebec fly 3,000 km south to Mexico every autumn. When they arrive there in October, they roost in huge swarms in the mountain forests, where they spend the winter.

At the beginning of March, they start to migrate north once more, flying at about 18 km an hour. As they travel, the females pause to lay eggs on milkweed plants. When the eggs hatch, and after the caterpillars have pupated, the newly-emerged adults continue the journey north.

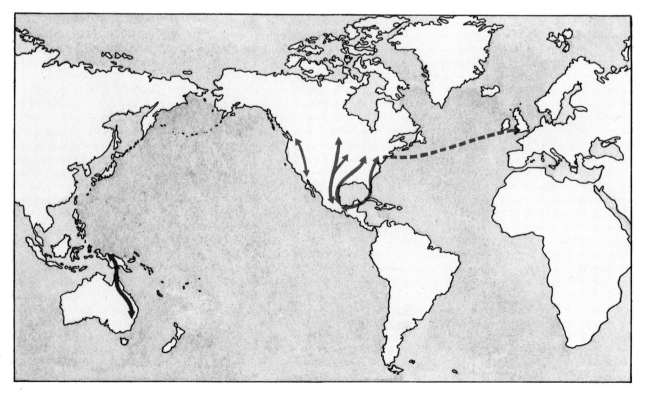

From May to August, monarchs breed on milkweed plants near the Great Lakes in Canada. In September, the survivors fly south again all the way to Mexico.

This journey was a mystery until a Canadian professor found a way of marking the butterflies with tiny sticky paper labels. When he went to Mexico, he found some of the butterflies which he had marked in Canada.

Although very few other butterflies make such long direct flights as the monarch, most species which live in temperate areas drift to cooler places in spring, and return towards the equator in autumn. They pause to feed and breed on suitable plants as they go. Well-known examples are the red admiral, painted lady and clouded yellow, which in summer fly to parts of northern Europe from as far south as North Africa.

Newly-arrived monarchs settle in a Mexican forest.

The diagram below shows different beak markings of two Bewick's swans.

Swans with names

At first sight, one swan looks much like another. If we look at them more closely, however, there is a sure way to tell them apart.

The method of identifying swans was discovered at The Wildfowl Trust, Slimbridge, Gloucestershire, in the west of England. Sir Peter Scott, the famous naturalist, found that he could recognize individual Bewick's swans by the patterns on their bills. He gave the birds names. From then on, it was possible to follow their family life when the swans came back from their breeding-grounds in Siberia every autumn.

Now we know that the pairs stay together for life, and that they live at least 25 years. The parents bring the young swans with them when they leave Siberia.

A pair of Bewick's swans on a Siberian lake in summer.

The family stays together during the first winter. In February they return together to Siberia, flying across Europe. On the way, the swans meet others which have spent the winter in Ireland, or elsewhere in Britain. They gather in favourite stopping-places, where they can rest and feed before flying on to Siberia.

As they fly from the Netherlands to West Germany and onwards across Eastern Europe, the swans become the responsibiity of one country after another. The birds themselves are protected by law everywhere they go, but it is just as important to protect the estuaries and marshes which they need as resting-places on the way.

There are other swans which migrate in a similar way in North America, and they probably share a similar family life. So far, however, nobody has found out how to tell them apart in the same way as is used for the Bewick's swans at the Wildfowl Trust in Slimbridge.

15

Herds of the frozen North

Around the Arctic Circle in Scandinavia, Siberia, Canada and Alaska live huge herds of reindeer, or caribou. They are the same species, called 'caribou' in North America and 'reindeer' in Europe and Asia. Around the Arctic Circle, winters are long and very cold, and summers are brief. During the winter, the deer shelter in the forests to the south of the Arctic Circle, but they migrate to the north for the summer, to graze on the tundra.

Caribou travel as much as 1,000 km in each direction. The females lead the way, beginning in early spring. They walk about 450 km until they reach one of their regular calving-grounds, where they give birth. On these wild, exposed hillsides they are safer from predators.

When the calves are born, the herd moves on. By now the males and young caribou from previous years have caught up with the main herd.

A caribou herd grazes on the tundra as snow melts in the Arctic summer. With them are two young Lapp herders wearing traditional dress.

A Lapp herder in a boat leads caribou across water to their summer pastures in the north of Norway.

The calves can run a few hours after they are born, and the herd moves quickly to the far northern pastures. There they feed on the tundra plants, such as mosses and lichens.

By September, the tundra begins to freeze again, the plants die off, and the caribou must move into the forests once more. There the deep snow is soft enough for them to find food underneath.

In Lapland, reindeer are traditionally followed by nomadic tribes called Lapps, who move with them along the migratory journey. They protect the animals from bears and wolves, and make use of their milk, skins and meat.

Herds of the African plains

The great herds of wildebeest, zebra and Thomson's gazelle which live on the African plains migrate in search of fresh grass to eat. During the dry season, they feed in open woodlands near Lake Victoria, but when the rainy season begins in December, they move out on to the open grasslands of the Serengeti Plain. For the next three months they wander round the plain, always moving towards places where rain is falling, to eat the fresh, young grass. Sometimes they follow thunder clouds as much as 100 km away.

The grass which springs up in the rainy season lasts the herds for another three months, until the plains become too dry. In June, they migrate back to the woodlands by the lake, where the grass has recovered and there is still plenty of water.

Further to the north, in the Sudan, another migration occurs. During the rainy season, the River Nile floods. Enormous herds of kob antelope are driven south, as the water spreads 800 km across the plain.

When the rains stop, the kob move slowly northwards again. They follow the flooded area, feeding on the grass which grows as the land dries. As the huge herds move northwards, they can find fresh grass every day. Later in the dry season, when the grass has all been eaten, the kob must move south again, to meet the approaching rains. Like wildebeest, they gallop towards every thunder cloud they can see or hear. Soon the rainy season starts, the river overflows, and the kob are driven far to the south to begin all over again.

On the Serengeti Plain in Africa, herds of wildebeest follow rain clouds to find fresh grass.

The rare whooping crane

A whooping crane egg is placed in the nest of a sandhill crane in Idaho, USA.

Every autumn, a small flock of whooping cranes arrives at Aransas, on the coast of Texas, USA. There are only about one hundred of them left. They became so rare because the marshes where they nested were drained and made into farmland. Until 1955 their remaining breeding place was a mystery. Then it was discovered, in Alberta, north-western Canada. At that time there were only twenty-one birds alive. Since then, their numbers have increased very slowly and the birds have a safe home in Wood Buffalo National Park, Alberta.

The reason for their slow recovery is that they are very special migrants. They will nest only in the area where their parents take them on their first migratory flight, nearly 4,000 km from Canada to Texas. Although there are other suitable breeding and wintering places, the cranes will not use them.

Another unusual feature of whooping cranes is that, although they lay two eggs, one of their chicks always dies in its first two weeks of life. To make the cranes safer, scientists took one egg from each of twelve nests in Canada, and put them in the nests of sandhill cranes, which breed in Idaho, in the northern USA. They hoped that each sandhill crane would look after the whooping crane chick as if it were its own.

Sandhill cranes migrate as well, but only a little over 1,000 km, to New Mexico. When the baby whooping cranes hatched and grew up, they followed the sandhill cranes on their migration. Now there are two populations of this rare and beautiful bird.

Opposite *Some whooping cranes in the marshes of Aransas, Texas. The birds arrive each autumn in order to spend the winter there.*

The migratory route of the whooping crane from Canada to Texas

Migrating fish

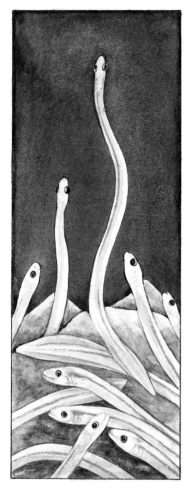

A group of young Sargasso eels.

Salmon hatch in fresh water, but they migrate to the sea when they are about 10 cm long. How old they are depends on where they live. In Britain they leave at about one-year-old, but in northern Canada or Norway it may take them eight years.

Salmon spend up to four years at sea. Salmon from many different rivers mingle together, but when the time comes to return to fresh water to breed, each goes to the river where it hatched, and even to the same patch of gravel. They recognize the place by its smell, which they remember from when they were babies.

Salmon from the Pacific Ocean die when they have bred once, but Atlantic salmon, especially in Canada, may survive to return to sea and breed again in the following season.

Eels live in just the opposite way. They hatch in the Sargasso Sea in the western Atlantic, and migrate to fresh water when they are old enough. There are two separate species in the Sargasso. The North American eel leaves to find fresh water when it is one-year-old, while the European eel stays at sea for three years.

Young eels are transparent. When they first swim up rivers they are called elvers. When they are six or seven years old they turn silver. Now they are ready to leave and return to the Sargasso Sea to breed.

The bluefin tuna fish, or tunnyfish, migrates great distances in search of food. Scientists have tagged them and traced their journey from the waters off Florida and the Bahamas, where they spawn in June, up to Nova Scotia, some 2,500 km north.

Opposite *Two salmon leap up a waterfall as they return to their freshwater breeding ground from the sea.*

Marine mammals

A grey whale surfaces near Vancouver Island, Canada.

Humpback whales spend the polar summer around the North or South Pole, feeding on the mass of krill in the sea. When the summer ends, however, the water soon freezes over, so the whales must leave. They migrate almost 5000 km from the Poles to warmer tropical waters, where they breed. They return to polar waters when summer begins again. The two populations of humpback whales never meet because when one is in tropical waters avoiding a polar winter, the other is enjoying summer at the other pole.

There is only one population of grey whales. They spend the summer in the Arctic, and migrate down the west coast of the USA to Mexico for the winter.

There they gather in sheltered lagoons to mate and produce their calves. The round trip of about 20,000 km takes roughly three months each way.

Seals migrate as well, but those which breed in temperate places do not travel very far. Monk seals and grey seals wander away from their breeding beaches to moult, and to feed for a few months. Southern elephant seals, on the other hand, breed on Antarctic islands and migrate as far as 2,000 km northwards to feed in winter. Sometimes the seals reach western Australia.

The walrus is rather unusual. Its pups are born in May on an ice floe and they stay with their mother for as long as three years, occasionally moving to a nearby floe. The ice drifts with the changing currents, and the walruses are carried on a circular route which may be as much as 1,000 km long.

A scene from the Falkland Islands in the South Atlantic Ocean, where the Antarctic fur seal (left) and the southern elephant seal (right) migrate to breed.

Fuel for the journey

Some animals must migrate in order to find food, and others must find food in order to migrate. In the first group, wildebeest and caribou travel from place to place in search of fresh grass, feeding as they go. Kob antelope in the Sudan are different – on their journey south they must cross a dry area where there is no grass to eat. To survive, they must have fed well before leaving the good grass of the north.

Long-distance sea bird migrants, including the arctic tern, can feed wherever they are. However, the polar waters where they spend the summer are much richer in food than the sea near the equator, which they must cross twice a year.

Salmon stop feeding when they return to fresh water. They must be fat and healthy when they leave the sea, especially if they are to return to it again after breeding.

Land birds such as thrushes or swallows must feed themselves up before they cross deserts or make long sea crossings. Geese are water birds, but they cannot feed on the sea, so they too must fatten up before they leave the land.

Each spring several species of hummingbird fly across the Gulf of Mexico to nest in western parts of the USA. They return to South America in the autumn. Scientists have found that the tiny birds cannot store enough fat to make the 3,000 km trip. The birds solve the problem by flying very high, where there are air currents which help to speed them on their way.

Scientists are learning more and more, but some of the wonders of migration may never be explained. One important lesson is that migratory animals need protection in all the countries along the route of their amazing journeys.

Opposite *The black-chinned hummingbird (top left), ruby-throated hummingbird (top right) and rufous hummingbird (below) all migrate from South America to the western USA. They are shown feeding on hibiscus flowers.*

Glossary

Arctic Circle An imaginary circle around the world that passes through Alaska, Canada, Greenland, Norway, Finland and Russia, which divides the frozen north from the warmer south.

Artificial Unnatural or man-made.

Bedouin Nomadic Arab peoples who live in the deserts of Arabia, Jordan, Syria and in the Sahara.

Compass An instrument for finding direction with a needle that always points to magnetic north.

Estuary The wide part of a river where it flows into the sea.

Floe A floating piece of flat ice.

Hibernate To sleep through the winter.

Krill Small shrimp-like creatures of the oceans.

Lapland The name for the area north of the Arctic Circle that includes parts of Norway, Sweden, Finland and Russia.

Magnetic Field The field of force around a magnet and around the earth.

Moult To shed old hairs or feathers, and grow new ones.

Navigate To find one's way.

Nomadic Wandering, with no fixed home.

Northern Hemisphere The northern half of the earth.

Oasis (pl. oases) A watering place in a desert.

Planetarium A building which recreates the movement of the sun, moon and stars. These are imitated by shining lights on to a domed ceiling.

Plankton The many different tiny animals and plants which spend all or part of their lives drifting near the surface of the sea.

Predator An animal which kills other animals for food.

Pupate To change from a caterpillar to a pupa (chrysalis), which will split to produce an adult.

Roost To find a safe place to sleep. Usually used of birds, but also of some insects, such as mosquitoes.

Southern Hemisphere The southern half of the earth.

Temperate The parts of the earth between polar and tropical regions are called the temperate zones.

Transparent Clear, see-through.

Tundra The grasslands beyond the northernmost trees in the Arctic.

Picture Acknowledgements

The publishers would like to thank those who provided photographs for this book:
Bryan and Cherry Alexander 17; Bruce Coleman Limited 20 (Jeff Foott); Survival Anglia Limited 9 and 27 (Jeff Foott), 22 (Cindy Buxton/Annie Price).

Further information

You can find out more about migration by reading the following books:

Animal Worlds, T. Rowland-Entwistle and Jean Cooke (Sampson Low, 1974)

Animals that Travel, Gwynne Vevers (Bodley Head, 1981)

Atlas of Animal Migration, Cathy Jarman (Heinemann, 1972)

Gak-Gak, Benny Gensbøl (Wayland, 1978)

How Birds Behave, Neil Ardley (Hamlyn, 1971)

Lapps, Reindeer Herders of Lapland, Alan James (Wayland, 1986)

Migrating Birds, Klaus Ruge (Hart-Davis, 1981)

Reindeer, Ewan Clarkson (Wayland, 1981)

The Sixth Sense of Animals, Maurice Burton (J M Dent, 1973)

Whales and Dolphins, Terence Wise (Wayland, 1983)

Some of the wildlife films that are shown on television follow animals on their migrations. You may find that some birds regularly fly to a breeding ground in your country, or that other birds fly over your local area while on their way elsewhere. You may also like to join an organization which helps to protect wild animals from extinction. Some useful addresses are:

The Royal Society for the Protection of Birds
The Lodge
Sandy
Bedfordshire SG19 2DL
England

The Royal Society for Nature Conservation
The Green
Nettleham
Lincoln LN2 2NR
(The Society runs a junior club called 'Watch')

World Wildlife Fund (Australia)
Level 17
St Martin's Tower
31 Market Street
GPO Box 528
Sydney NSW 2001

World Wildlife Fund (UK)
Panda House
11–13 Ockford Road
Godalming
Surrey

World Wildlife Fund (USA)
1255 23rd Street
Washington DC 20037

Greenpeace (UK)
36 Graham Street
London NW 8LL

Greenpeace (USA)
1611 Connecticut Avenue N.W.
Washington DC 2009

Greenpeace (Australia)
310 Angas Street
Adelaide 5000

Index